PRESENTS

T0163643

Meet the

Parts
of
Speech

8
POPULATION

Student Workbook

FIRST GRADE

written by
THE MAYOR OF GRAMMAROPOLIS

HOUSTON

Edited by Christopher Knight
Cover and Interior Design by Mckee Frazior
Character Design by Powerhouse Animation

ISBN: 9781644420300
Copyright © 2020 by Grammaropolis LLC
Illustrations copyright © 2020 by Grammaropolis LLC
All rights reserved.
Published by Grammaropolis
Distributed by Six Foot Press
Printed in the U.S.A.

Grammaropolis.com
SixFootPress.com

Table of Contents

Grammaropolis

Table of Contents

For information on how Grammaropolis correlates to state standards, please visit us online at edu.grammaropolis.com

FROM THE DESK OF THE MAYOR

There's a reason students can instantly recall everything that happened in their favorite movies but struggle to retain much of the important information you're trying to cover in school: people are hard-wired to remember what we connect with on an emotional level.

That's why grammar is so hard to teach. (As a former grammar teacher myself, I know firsthand.) Traditional materials are dry, abstract, and lifeless. There's nothing to connect with. Put simply, grammar is boring.

But it doesn't have to be! Our story-based approach combines traditional instruction with original narrative content, appealing to different learning styles and encouraging students to make a deeper connection with the elements of grammar.

In Grammaropolis, adverbs don't just modify verbs; adverbs are bossy! They tell the verbs **where** to go, **when** to leave, and **how** to get there. A pronoun doesn't just replace a noun; Roger the pronoun is a shady character who's always trying to trick Nelson the noun into giving up his spot.

And it works! Our mobile apps have already been downloaded over 2.5 million times, and thousands of schools and districts use our web-based site license. In other words, we don't skimp on the vegetables; we just make them taste good.

Thanks so much for visiting Grammaropolis. I hope you enjoy your stay!

– The Mayor

Meet the Parts of Speech!

Nouns

name a person, place, thing, or idea.

Verbs

express action or a state of being.

Adverbs

tell how, when, or where an action happens.

Adjectives

modify a noun or pronoun.

Prepositions

locate an object in time or space.

Pronouns

take the place of one or more nouns or pronouns.

Interjections

express strong or mild emotion.

Conjunctions

join words or word groups.

Meet the Parts of Speech, Grade 1 © 2020 by Grammaropo...

EXAMPLES

PERSON: <u>Devin</u> gave his <u>**mom**</u> a hug.

PLACE: People love to visit <u>**New Mexico**</u>.

THING: Julian put his <u>**sandwich**</u> on a <u>**plate**</u>.

IDEA: I wish you nothing but <u>**happiness**</u>.

A Noun Names a Person

A noun can name a person.

My **grandmother** took me shopping for new shoes.

Mr. Johnson is the best!

Let's practice!

Instructions:
Circle any noun that names a person in each of the following sentences.

EXAMPLE:

(Kyla) jumped over the sidewalk.

1. Please give Sandra a pencil.

2. Albert and Jacob enjoy the rain.

3. Don't tell your mother about the surprise party!

4. That girl is great at soccer.

5. Your teacher is funny.

Your turn!

Instructions:
Use the nouns below to write your very own sentences.
Don't forget to circle the nouns when you use them!

1. fireman _____

2. Calla _____

3. uncle _____

Meet the Parts of Speech, Grade 1 © 2020 by Grammaropo[lis]

A Noun Names a Place

A noun can name a place.

This **zoo** has so many wonderful animals.

Lizzie enjoys learning about **South America**.

Let's practice!

Instructions:
Circle any noun that names a place in each of the following sentences.

EXAMPLE:

Julian and his sister went to the (park.)

1. That hotel has comfortable beds.

2. What is your favorite city to visit in the summertime?

3. Marcus went to the hospital to learn about medicine.

4. Most restaurants in Paris serve baguettes.

5. Jamie left his homework at home.

Your turn!

Instructions:
Use the nouns below to write your very own sentences. Don't forget to circle the nouns when you use them!

1. school _____

2. New York _____

3. bedroom _____

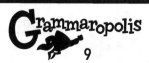

A Noun Names a Thing

Let's practice!

Instructions:
Circle any noun that names a thing in each of the following sentences. (There may be more than one!)

EXAMPLE:
Someone should write a new (book) about (seahorses.)

1. I jumped on the trampoline until I was exhausted.

2. Enrique gave his teacher a big green apple.

3. Kellie forgot to bring her ball today.

4. Put your pencil on the table and close your eyes.

5. Her dog loves to eat strawberries.

Your turn!

Instructions:
Use the nouns below to write your very own sentences. Don't forget to circle the nouns when you use them!

1. computer _____

2. lion _____

3. grapefruit _____

Meet the Parts of Speech, Grade 1 © 2020 by Grammaropo

A Noun Names an Idea

A noun can name an idea, which you can't perceive with one or more of your five senses.

I want you to fight for **truth** and **justice**!

Pro Tip:
A noun that names an idea is called an **abstract noun**.

Let's practice!

Instructions:
Circle any noun that names an idea in each of the following sentences.

EXAMPLE:

Tina showed me wonderful kindness when I skinned my knee.

1. The Beatles said, "All you need is love."

2. Teachers must have a lot of patience.

3. You should always pay attention to your parents.

4. Sheldon wants to learn more humility.

5. Gabriel's friendship is very important to me.

Your turn!

Instructions:
Use the nouns below to write your very own sentences. Don't forget to circle the nouns when you use them!

1. sadness _____

2. honesty _____

3. joy _____

Common Nouns & Proper Nouns

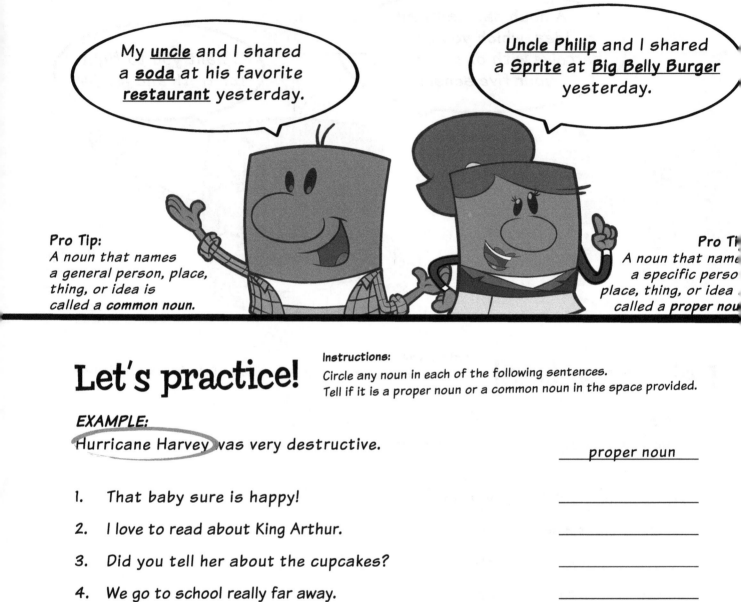

My **uncle** and I shared a **soda** at his favorite **restaurant** yesterday.

Uncle Philip and I shared a **Sprite** at **Big Belly Burger** yesterday.

Pro Tip:
A noun that names a general person, place, thing, or idea is called a **common noun**.

Pro Ti
A noun that name
a specific perso
place, thing, or idea
called a **proper nou**

Let's practice!

Instructions:
Circle any noun in each of the following sentences.
Tell if it is a proper noun or a common noun in the space provided.

EXAMPLE:

Hurricane Harvey was very destructive.   ___proper noun___

1. That baby sure is happy!   _____

2. I love to read about King Arthur.   _____

3. Did you tell her about the cupcakes?   _____

4. We go to school really far away.   _____

5. Henry would like to know how you feel about it.   _____

Your turn!

Instructions:
Write a sentence that includes a proper noun, a sentence that includes a common noun, and a sentence that includes at least one of each. Don't forget to circle the nouns!

1. proper   _____

2. common   _____

3. one of each _____

Meet the Parts of Speech, Grade 1 © 2020 by Grammaropol*

Singular Nouns & Plural Nouns

Julie spotted a **shark** swimming way out in the **ocean**.

Do you know how many **sharks** there are in all the **oceans** on the planet?

Pro Tip:
A singular noun names a single person, place, thing, or idea.

Pro Tip:
A plural noun names more than one person, place, thing, or idea.

Let's Practice!

Instructions:
In each of the following sentences, circle any singular nouns and underline any plural nouns.

EXAMPLE:
Salamanders have such sticky feet that they can climb up glass.

1. Will you please bring me another plate?

2. Sally remembered turn in her papers before the bell rang.

3. Tomatoes are more nutritious than many people think.

4. Can you give Erika a pencil?

5. Dayton always puts his name on his shoes.

Your turn!

Instructions:
Turn the following singular nouns into plural nouns!

tooth	_____	city	_____
kiss	_____	key	_____
pizza	_____	radio	_____
lady	_____	rule	_____

Meet the Parts of Speech, Grade 1 © 2020 by Grammaropolis

Noun Journal

INSTRUCTIONS:
Keeping track of great words is more fun than you might think!
Write down your favorite nouns for each of these categories.

PERSON

These are your favorite nouns that name a person. They can be proper nouns or common nouns.

coach _____   _____   _____

_____   _____   _____

_____   _____   _____

PLACE

These are your favorite nouns that name a place. They can be proper nouns or common nouns.

cave _____   _____   _____

_____   _____   _____

_____   _____   _____

THING

These are your favorite nouns that name a thing. They can be singular nouns or plural nouns.

buckles _____   _____   _____

_____   _____   _____

_____   _____   _____

IDEA

These are your favorite nouns that name an idea. Remember that these nouns can't be perceived by any of the five senses.

joy _____   _____   _____

_____   _____   _____

_____   _____   _____

These will come in handy on the next page!

Grammaropolis

Meet the Parts of Speech, Grade 1 © 2020 by Grammarop

Writing with Nouns

INSTRUCTIONS:
Select a few nouns from your Noun Journal and write them in the spaces provided.

PERSON	PLACE	THING	IDEA
----------------------	----------------------	----------------------	----------------------
----------------------	----------------------	----------------------	----------------------
----------------------	----------------------	----------------------	----------------------

INSTRUCTIONS (PART TWO):
Now write sentences using some of the nouns you've selected. (Of course, now that you're a noun expert, you don't have to limit yourself to the nouns from your journal.) Be sure to circle any of the nouns you use!

1. _____

2. _____

3. _____

4. _____

5. _____

6. _____

Meet the Parts of Speech, Grade 1 © 2020 by Grammaropolis

The Big Noun Quiz!

INSTRUCTIONS: Identify the noun in each of the sentences below from the available options.

1. The wind shook the tree branches outside my window.
    - ○ shook
    - ○ wind
    - ○ outside
    - ○ my

2. Sarwah's friends hired a band to play at his birthday party.
    - ○ band
    - ○ play
    - ○ his
    - ○ hired

3. The menu features cheeses from many different countries.
    - ○ many
    - ○ has
    - ○ cheeses
    - ○ different

4. A piercing ray of sunshine shone through the old library.
    - ○ shone
    - ○ sunshine
    - ○ old
    - ○ through

5. The smell of freshly cut grass filled the park in the morning.
    - ○ freshly
    - ○ filled
    - ○ in
    - ○ grass

INSTRUCTIONS: Is the underlined noun in each of the sentences below a common noun or proper noun?

6. Franklin promised to finish the book on <u>Sunday</u>.
    - ○ common noun
    - ○ proper noun

7. I had a dream about the <u>festival</u> the night before it happened.
    - ○ common noun
    - ○ proper noun

8. Visitors are welcome to tour the <u>school</u> on weekdays.
    - ○ common noun
    - ○ proper noun

9. That hat belongs to my cousin <u>Bernice</u>.
    - ○ common noun
    - ○ proper noun

10. We all studied <u>Spanish</u> before our trip to Mexico.
    - ○ common noun
    - ○ proper noun

Grammaropolis

16

Meet the Parts of Speech, Grade 1 © 2020 by Grammaropo[lis]

Meet the Verbs!

I am an action verb!

I express action.

EXAMPLES

They **play** basketball.
Mandy **ate** a pear.
Bill **walked**.

I am a linking verb.

I express a state of being.

EXAMPLES

My penguin **is** cold.
That apple **was** red.
She **looks** sad.

Action Verbs Express Action

Seema _ran_ home.

I **remember** something important!

Pro Tip:
An action verb can express either **physical** action or **mental** action.

Let's practice!

Instructions:
Circle the action verb in each of the following sentences and indicate whether it is expressing physical or mental action.

EXAMPLE:

Harry's dog (shook) water all over us.   ___physical action___

1.   Please organize your locker.   _____

2.   Marion prefers chocolate shakes.   _____

3.   All of Jaime's friends shop here!   _____

4.   The lightning bolt destroyed Antonio's computer. _____

5.   Sophie imagined a world without ice cream.   _____

Your turn!

Instructions:
Write sentences using your own action verbs to express mental or physical action as indicated. Don't forget to circle the action verb you use!

1.   physical _____

2.   mental _____

3.   physical _____

Action Verbs Express Physical Action

Kylie **_climbed_** to the top of the fence and then **_jumped_** all the way down.

Pro Tip:
When an action verb expresses physical action, it tells what a noun or pronoun **did**, **does**, or **will do**.

Let's practice!

Instructions:
Circle all of the action verbs expressing physical action in each of the following sentences.

EXAMPLE:
Jeremy (slipped) on the banana peel.

1. Tyra sings beautifully.

2. She baked her brother a cake for his birthday.

3. Riley and Stefan acted in the school play.

4. A dog followed Mila home last night.

5. Ethan knocked quietly on Old Man Garcia's front door.

Your turn!

Instructions:
Write three sentences using action verbs of your own to express physical action. Don't forget to circle each of the action verbs you use!

1. _____

2. _____

3. _____

Meet the Parts of Speech, Grade 1 © 2020 by Grammaropolis

Action Verbs Express Mental Action

Because I **studied** for my exams,
I **thought** that I would do well.

Pro Tip:
When a verb expresses
mental action, the action is
not visible.

Let's practice!

Instructions:
Circle all of the action verbs expressing mental action in each of the following sentences.

EXAMPLE:
Tomás (wonders) what his brother (believes.)

1. They dreamed about pumpkin pie.

2. I love strawberry ice cream.

3. Jackie remembered her homework.

4. Felix knew all the answers.

5. Daphne's sister hopes for rain tomorrow.

Your turn!

Instructions:
Write three sentences using action verbs of your own to express mental action. Don't forget to circle each of the action verbs you use!

1. _____

2. _____

3. _____

Meet the Parts of Speech, Grade 1 © 2020 by Grammaropolis

Linking Verbs Express a State of Being

Let's practice!

Instructions:
Circle the linking verb in each of the following sentences.

EXAMPLE:
The other team was great at soccer.

1. Your room smells funny.

2. My friend Jason became a professor of English.

3. I am so proud of you!

4. The tomato soup tasted delicious.

5. We were sad during the movie.

Your turn!

Instructions:
Write three sentences using your own linking verbs. Make sure one of the sentences uses a linking verb that is not a form of "to be." Don't forget to circle the linking verbs!

1. _____

2. _____

3. _____

Action Verb or Linking Verb?

Linking Verb:
Frankie's hamburger **tasted** delicious!

Action Verb:
Frankie **tasted** onions and garlic in her hamburger.

Pro Tip:
Some words can be action verbs or linking verbs depending on how they're used.

Let's practice!

Instructions:
Circle the verb in each of the following sentences and indicate whether it is an action verb or a linking verb.

EXAMPLE:

My shirt (smelled) terrible after my bicycle ride.   linking verb

1. Andrew stayed angry with me.   _____

2. Luna stayed at my house last night.   _____

3. Eduardo sounded the fire alarm!   _____

4. I felt sick after the party.   _____

5. Mrs. Norwood's class grew tomato plants for a project.   _____

Your turn!

Instructions:
Write sentences using the verbs below as action verbs or linking verbs as indicated. Don't forget to circle the verb in the sentence!

1. smell (action) _____

2. smell (linking) _____

3. feel (action) _____

Meet the Parts of Speech, Grade 1 © 2020 by Grammaropo

Verb Tenses

A **past tense** verb tells about an action or state of being that already happened in the past. (Most past tense verbs end in -ed)

Past Tense:
Vinny <u>jumped</u> over the tree stump yesterday.

A **present tense** verb tells about an action or state of being in the present.

Present Tense:
Vinny <u>jumps</u> over the tree stump on his way to school.

A **future tense** verb tells about an action or state of being that will happen in the future.

Future Tense:
Vinny <u>will jump</u> over the tree stump tomorrow.

Let's practice!

Instructions:
Circle the verb in each of the following sentences and indicate whether it is in the present, past, or future tense.

EXAMPLE:

My little sister (shows) me the star constellations.   __present tense__

1.   Angela's mom will give us snacks.   _____

2.   People sure are friendly around here.   _____

3.   Maribel probably will accept my invitation.   _____

4.   That poor kitty slept outside all night.   _____

5.   I slammed the door loudly.   _____

Your turn!

Instructions:
Write three different sentences using the same verb in the past tense, present tense, and future tense. Don't forget to circle the verb!

1.   Past   _____

2.   Present   _____

3.   Future   _____

Irregular Past Tense Verbs

Dayton <u>left</u> as soon as the party was over.
I <u>heard</u> a noise in the middle of the night.
Letty <u>made</u> her teacher a birthday card.

leave → left
hear → heard
make → made

Pro Tip:
An irregular past tense verb is a past tense verb that is not formed by putting -d or -ed after the present tense verb.

Let's practice!

Instructions:
Circle the correct form of the past tense verb in parentheses.

EXAMPLE:

My brother (gived, gave) me an ice cream cone.

1. Unfortunately, we (lost, losed) the big game.

2. Blake and his sister (spended, spent) all their money.

3. Harmony (stuck, sticked) a sticker on Craig's book.

4. No matter what, Phoebe always (told, telled) the truth.

5. I (eated, ate) an enormous breakfast.

Your turn!

Instructions:
Write down the correct past tense verb form for each of the present tense verbs below.

say	_____	stand	_____	throw	_____
sleep	_____	make	_____	steal	_____
run	_____	teach	_____	sit	_____

Meet the Parts of Speech, Grade 1 © 2020 by Grammaropo[lis]

Writing with Verbs

INSTRUCTIONS (PART ONE):
Brainstorm some of your favorite action verbs and linking verbs. Make different lists for action verbs that express physical action and action verbs that express mental action

PHYSICAL ACTION VERB	MENTAL ACTION VERB	LINKING VERB
-------------------------------	-------------------------------	-------------------------------
-------------------------------	-------------------------------	-------------------------------
-------------------------------	-------------------------------	-------------------------------
-------------------------------	-------------------------------	-------------------------------

INSTRUCTIONS (PART TWO):
Now choose TWO verbs from each of your categories and use them to write sentences in the spaces below. Don't forget to circle the verbs!

_____

_____

_____

_____

_____

_____

Meet the Parts of Speech, Grade 1 © 2020 by Grammaropolis

The Big Verb Quiz!

INSTRUCTIONS: Identify the verb in each of the sentences below.

1. The cat was curious about everything.
    - ○ curious
    - ○ cat
    - ○ was
    - ○ The

2. The boats in the harbor sailed into the bay.
    - ○ sailed
    - ○ harbor
    - ○ into
    - ○ bay

3. Herman feels proud of his work.
    - ○ proud
    - ○ work
    - ○ feels
    - ○ Herman

4. Pizza is my favorite food.
    - ○ food
    - ○ favorite
    - ○ Pizza
    - ○ is

5. Magdalena went to the store for some milk.
    - ○ went
    - ○ for
    - ○ store
    - ○ milk

6. That pigeon flew right into the window!
    - ○ pigeon
    - ○ That
    - ○ flew
    - ○ window

7. Andrei's pet hedgehog knows many tricks.
    - ○ knows
    - ○ hedgehog
    - ○ pet
    - ○ tricks

8. Don't give me that attitude, young lady!
    - ○ lady
    - ○ young
    - ○ attitude
    - ○ give

9. The hiking trail will be muddy after the rain.
    - ○ hiking
    - ○ will be
    - ○ after
    - ○ trail

10. Cora tied her shoes with double knots.
    - ○ tied
    - ○ double
    - ○ with
    - ○ her

Meet the Adjectives!

EXAMPLES

WHAT KIND: I only wear <u>purple</u> shoes on Tuesdays.

WHICH ONE: My dad always sits in the <u>front</u> row.

HOW MANY: I would like <u>seven</u> chocolate bars.

HOW MUCH: Please give me <u>more</u> chocolate.

Using Adjectives to Describe

Julia and the <u>older</u> students waited together in the <u>crowded</u> lobby.

Pro Tip:
An adjective describes one or more nouns or pronouns. It can tell **what kind, which one, how many,** or **how much.**

Let's practice!

Instructions:
Circle all of the adjectives in each of the following sentences.

EXAMPLE:
There are (two)(stinky) apples on the counter.

1. Nick ate a huge breakfast.

2. The yellow cat ran away.

3. I picked a tiny green flower!

4. Eli gave me a wonderful, new book.

5. A quiet room is the best place for reading.

Your turn!

Instructions:
Write a sentence using adjectives to describe each of the nouns below. Don't forget to circle all the adjectives you use!

1. ball _____

2. dog _____

3. present _____

Adjectives and the Five Senses

I wandered into the **dark** woods.

That pear is **sweet**!

Pro Tip:
You can use your five senses
(taste, smell, touch, hear, see)
to describe nouns and
pronouns with adjectives.

Let's practice!

Instructions:
Circle all of the adjectives in each of the following sentences.

EXAMPLE:
Selma gave Tyrone an orange sweater.

1. Blankets can be warm.

2. There are seven tiny ducklings in here.

3. Tim lives in a noisy house.

4. The cookies you gave me are dry and stale.

5. The lunchroom smells terrible.

Your turn!

Instructions:
Write sentences using your five senses to come up with adjectives to describe each of the nouns below. Don't forget to circle all the adjectives you use!

1. sandwich _____

2. air _____

3. tree _____

Adjectives Can Tell "How Many" or "How Much"

How Many:
I ordered **_seven_** bowls of soup.

How Much:
I ordered **_more_** soup.

Pro Tip:
An adjective can tell
how many (a number or quantity)
or **how much** (an amount).

Let's practice!

Instructions:
Circle the adjective in each of the following sentences and indicate whether it is telling "how many" or "how much".

EXAMPLE:

(Six) people in my family believe in ghosts. ⎯⎯ how many ⎯⎯

1. Mary saved money for six months. ⎯⎯⎯⎯⎯⎯⎯⎯

2. There are many ways to build a house. ⎯⎯⎯⎯⎯⎯⎯⎯

3. A cyclops has one eye. ⎯⎯⎯⎯⎯⎯⎯⎯

4. We were attacked by seventeen llamas! ⎯⎯⎯⎯⎯⎯⎯⎯

5. Two swans swam elegantly across the lake. ⎯⎯⎯⎯⎯⎯⎯⎯

Your turn!

Instructions:
Write a sentence using each of the words below as an adjective describing how many or how much. Don't forget to circle the adjectives!

1. some ⎯⎯⎯⎯⎯⎯⎯⎯⎯⎯⎯⎯⎯⎯⎯⎯⎯⎯⎯⎯⎯⎯

2. twelve ⎯⎯⎯⎯⎯⎯⎯⎯⎯⎯⎯⎯⎯⎯⎯⎯⎯⎯⎯⎯⎯

3. more ⎯⎯⎯⎯⎯⎯⎯⎯⎯⎯⎯⎯⎯⎯⎯⎯⎯⎯⎯⎯⎯⎯

Meet the Parts of Speech, Grade 1 © 2020 by Grammaropolis

Words Adjectives Modify

Adjectives before:

The <u>clear</u> water twinkled in the <u>morning</u> sunlight.

Adjectives after:

Kyle was so <u>nervous</u> before the game.

Pro Tip:
An adjective can come **before** or **after** the word or words it modifies.

Let's Practice!

Instructions:
Circle all of the adjectives in each of the following sentences.
Then draw an arrow from each adjective to the word it modifies.

EXAMPLE:
I am excited that the new restaurant opens tomorrow.

1. The students are ready.

2. Zingbat Cola is way too sugary.

3. Ron carved a beautiful jack-o-lantern.

4. I want to pick more purple flowers.

5. Read me a bedtime story!

Your turn!

Instructions:
Write sentences using the adjectives below to describe a noun or pronoun. Circle each adjective and draw an arrow to the word it modifies.

1. small _____

2. happy _____

3. golden _____

More Words Adjectives Modify

Adjectives before:

The **young** pony shook its **bushy** tail.

Adjectives after:

Nina looked really **tired** yesterday.

Pro Tip:
An adjective can come **before** or **after** the word or words it modifies.

Let's Practice!

Instructions:
Circle all of the adjectives in each of the following sentences.
Then draw an arrow from each adjective to the word it modifies.

EXAMPLE:
The new chef will teach you how to make fresh sushi.

1. The farmer feels close to nature.

2. Molly has an old dog.

3. Granny has fond memories of school.

4. The little park is peaceful at night.

5. Helen sings in the shower every morning.

Your turn!

Instructions:
Write sentences using the adjectives below to describe a noun or pronoun. Circ
each adjective and draw an arrow to the word it modifies.

1. snowy   _____

2. funny   _____

3. ready   _____

Even More Words Adjectives Modify

Adjectives before:

Mary had a <u>little</u> lamb.

Adjectives after:

Its fleece was <u>white</u> as snow.

Pro Tip:
An adjective can come **before** or **after** the word or words it modifies.

Let's Practice!

Instructions:
Circle all of the adjectives in each of the following sentences.
Then draw an arrow from each adjective to the word it modifies.

EXAMPLE:
I used (silver) paint today.

1. Phoebe wants to sit in the front seat.

2. Look into the magic mirror!

3. The mirror is magic!

4. Patricia left her loud parrot at home.

5. We feel ready for the difficult test.

Your turn!

Instructions:
Write sentences using the adjectives below to describe a noun or pronoun. Circle each adjective and draw an arrow to the word it modifies.

1. tall _____

2. round _____

3. huge _____

Meet the Parts of Speech, Grade 1 © 2020 by Grammaropolis

Using the Five Senses

INSTRUCTIONS:
Write down a list of adjectives you might use to describe things using each of your five senses.

SEE

purple _____ _____ _____

_____ _____ _____

HEAR

screechy _____ _____ _____

_____ _____ _____

SMELL

burnt _____ _____ _____

_____ _____ _____

TASTE

sweet _____ _____ _____

_____ _____ _____

TOUCH

soft _____ _____ _____

_____ _____ _____

These will come in handy on the next page!

Meet the Parts of Speech, Grade 1 © 2020 by Grammaropo

Writing with Adjectives

INSTRUCTIONS (PART ONE):

Brainstorm a list of adjectives you might use to describe each of the nouns below.

1. sandwich	2. shirt	3. gift	4. lake
----------------	----------------	----------------	----------------
----------------	----------------	----------------	----------------
----------------	----------------	----------------	----------------
----------------	----------------	----------------	----------------
----------------	----------------	----------------	----------------

INSTRUCTIONS (PART TWO):

Write sentences describing each of the nouns above using adjectives from your list. Circle the adjectives!

1. _____

2. _____

3. _____

4. _____

Meet the Parts of Speech, Grade 1 © 2020 by Grammaropolis

The Big Adjective Quiz!

INSTRUCTIONS: Identify the adjective in each of the sentences below from among the available options.

1. I will be ready to sing only after I take a nap.
   ○ after   ○ ready   ○ nap   ○ I

2. The campers ate fresh bread and cheese.
   ○ campers   ○ bread   ○ fresh   ○ ate

3. The children discovered a hidden garden yesterday.
   ○ hidden   ○ children   ○ yesterday   ○ garden

4. My parents make us sit through long family meetings.
   ○ parents   ○ meetings   ○ us   ○ long

5. Leila always takes time out of her busy schedule.
   ○ time   ○ busy   ○ schedule   ○ always

INSTRUCTIONS: Identify the word the <u>underlined adjective</u> modifies from among the available options.

6. A <u>slight</u> breeze tapped the branches against my window.
   ○ breeze   ○ branches   ○ window   ○ tapped

7. My dog is so incredibly <u>brave</u>!
   ○ My   ○ incredibly   ○ dog   ○ so

8. A full moon peeked out from behind the <u>misty</u> clouds.
   ○ moon   ○ clouds   ○ full   ○ behind

9. Some vegetables are very <u>expensive</u>.
   ○ vegetables   ○ are   ○ Some   ○ very

10. Your kitten's paws are <u>dirty</u> from being outside.
    ○ kitten's   ○ outside   ○ Your   ○ paws

Grammaropolis

36

Meet the Adverbs!

EXAMPLES

TELLING HOW: Speak <u>softly</u> and listen <u>closely</u>.

TELLING WHERE: Victor hurried <u>home</u>.

TELLING WHEN: The bake sale ends <u>tomorrow</u>.

Meet the Parts of Speech, Grade 1 © 2020 by Grammaropolis

Adverbs Can Tell "How"

Pro Tip:
*An adverb can tell **how** an action happens.*

Let's practice!

Instructions:
Circle all of the adverbs in each of the following sentences.

EXAMPLE:
Sharon will gladly eat your dessert.

1. Vicky tiptoed quietly across the carpet.

2. The principal talked supportively to us.

3. Duncan's grandfather hugged him tightly.

4. We ran happily toward the donut shop.

5. Mom filled the cups evenly.

Your turn!

Instructions:
Write sentences using the adverbs below to tell "how" an action happens. Don't forget to circle the adverbs!

1. quickly _____

2. slowly _____

3. angrily _____

Meet the Parts of Speech, Grade 1 © 2020 by Grammaropo...

Adverbs Can Tell "Where" or "When"

When:
Dany will *celebrate* her birthday <u>tomorrow</u>.

Where:
Come <u>here</u>!

Pro Tip:
An adverb can tell *where* or *when* an action happens.

Let's practice!

Instructions:
Circle the adverb in each of the following sentences and indicate whether it is telling "where" or "when" an action happens.

EXAMPLE:

The test is happening (today). _____ when _____

1. Please tell me a joke now. _____

2. I have looked everywhere. _____

3. Sebastian ran home. _____

4. Paula will do her homework later. _____

5. The apple fell nearby. _____

Your turn!

Instructions:
Write sentences using the adverbs below to tell "where" or "when" an action happens. Don't forget to circle the adverbs!

1. soon _____

2. yesterday _____

3. there _____

Words Adverbs Modify

Adverb before:

The postman **regularly** delivers the mail.

Adverb after:

The postman delivers the mail **regularly**.

Pro Ti
An adverb can con
before or **after** th
word it modifie

Let's practice!

Instructions:
Circle all of the adverbs in each of the following sentences.
Then draw an arrow from each adverb to the word it modifies.

EXAMPLE:
If you listened carefully, you definitely heard the owl.

1. The little girl lovingly hugged her baby doll.

2. The rain fell heavily that morning.

3. I never eat chocolate with peanut butter!

4. Kathie closed her backpack securely.

5. Hope completely finished her homework.

Your turn!

Instructions:
Write sentences using the adverbs below to describe a verb. Circle
each adverb and draw an arrow to the word it modifies.

1. quietly _____

2. always _____

3. nicely _____

Writing with Adverbs

INSTRUCTIONS (PART ONE):
Turn the following adjectives into adverbs by adding -ly to the end.

ADJECTIVE	ADVERB
1. clear	1.
2. strong	2.
3. slow	3.
4. glad	4.
5. soft	5.

INSTRUCTIONS (PART TWO):
Now write a sentence for each of your new adverbs. Remember to circle the adverb in the sentence and draw an arrow to the word it modifies.

_____

_____

_____

_____

_____

Meet the Parts of Speech, Grade 1 © 2020 by Grammaropolis

The Big Adverb Quiz!

INSTRUCTIONS: Identify the adverb in each of the sentences below from the available options.

1. Antonia sometimes forgets her telephone number.
   - ⭕ sometimes
   - ⭕ forgets
   - ⭕ number
   - ⭕ telephone

2. The mist sat heavily on the valley floor.
   - ⭕ sat
   - ⭕ valey
   - ⭕ heavily
   - ⭕ floor

3. Larry will undoubtedly pay what he owes.
   - ⭕ will
   - ⭕ undoubtedly
   - ⭕ Larry
   - ⭕ owes

4. Galina gazed longingly at the basket of fries.
   - ⭕ gazed
   - ⭕ basket
   - ⭕ fries
   - ⭕ longingly

5. The group sang together in a circle on the floor.
   - ⭕ sang
   - ⭕ group
   - ⭕ together
   - ⭕ floor

INSTRUCTIONS: Choose which of the available options is the word that the <u>underlined adverb</u> modifies.

6. Ethan read every single book <u>closely</u>.
   - ⭕ single
   - ⭕ read
   - ⭕ every
   - ⭕ book

7. Noel <u>immediately</u> recognized one of his favorite actors.
   - ⭕ Noel
   - ⭕ recognized
   - ⭕ favorite
   - ⭕ actors

8. Sergeant Avery <u>doggedly</u> searched for the lost necklace.
   - ⭕ the
   - ⭕ Sergeant
   - ⭕ searched
   - ⭕ necklace

9. The scarecrow smiled <u>mysteriously</u> as it swayed in the wind.
   - ⭕ smiled
   - ⭕ swayed
   - ⭕ wind
   - ⭕ scarecrow

10. The goalie secured the ball <u>tightly</u> in her hands.
    - ⭕ hands
    - ⭕ goalie
    - ⭕ tightly
    - ⭕ secured

Meet the Parts of Speech, Grade 1 © 2020 by Grammaropo

Meet the Pronouns!

I am a pronoun!

I take the place of one or more nouns or pronouns.

EXAMPLES

WITHOUT PRONOUNS: <u>Frederick</u> spilled <u>a jar</u> of mayonnaise on <u>my mother and father</u>.

WITH PRONOUNS: <u>He</u> spilled <u>it</u> on <u>them</u>.

Meet the Parts of Speech, Grade 1 © 2020 by Grammaropolis

Why We Use Pronouns

Without Pronouns:
Frank and Carl went to the store. Frank and Carl bought some cheese, and then Frank and Carl ate the cheese.

With Pronouns:
Frank and Carl went to the store. **They** bought some cheese, and then **they** ate **it**.

Pro Tip:
We use pronouns so that nouns or other pronouns in the sentence don't have to be repeated.

Let's practice!

Instructions:
Fill in the blanks in the sentences below using the pronouns from the word bank that make sense.

PRONOUN BANK:	it they her him them she we

EXAMPLE:

Whenever my mom smiles, __she__ makes me happy.

1. Alice's sisters are here. Let's say hello to _____.

2. Jimmy took my sandwich and ate ____.

3. Henry is coming. Don't tell _____ about the birthday surprise!

4. Pets are a lot of work. _____ have to be fed every day.

5. Bobby and I like ice cream, so _____ shared a big bowl of _____.

Your turn!

Instructions:
Write a short sentence using no pronouns. Then write the same sentence replacing the nouns with pronouns. Don't forget to circle the pronouns!

_____

_____

Meet the Parts of Speech, Grade 1 © 2020 by Grammaropo

Personal Pronouns

Pro Tip:
A personal pronoun takes the place of a person (and sometimes an animal or thing!).

Let's practice!

Instructions:
Circle the personal pronouns in the sentences below.

PERSONAL PRONOUNS: I me you we us he him it she her they them

EXAMPLE:

Miranda wants (me) to play the guitar for (her).

1. They always come over for dinner.

2. Does he really think we won't go to sleep?

3. You and I should definitely drink more water.

4. Tell Frankie that she is taking him to school.

5. I love movies about candy.

Your turn!

Instructions:
Write two sentences using personal pronouns. Don't forget to circle them!

_____

_____

Meet the Parts of Speech, Grade 1 © 2020 by Grammaropolis

Pronouns and Antecedents

Pro Tip:
The word (or words) that the pronoun replaces is called the antecedent.

Let's practice!

Instructions:
Circle the pronoun in each of the following sentences and draw an arrow to the word it replaces.

EXAMPLE:

Tom is a funny guy. He tells lots of jokes.

1. Tasha laughed so hard that she started crying.

2. Jacob is too loud. Please tell him to be quiet.

3. Jake ordered a hot sandwich, but it arrived cold.

4. Mom and Dad were sad because they got here late.

5. You and I are great artists. We should sell our paintings!

Your turn!

Instructions:
Write sentences using the word pairs below as the pronoun and antecedent. Then circle the pronoun and draw an arrow to the antecedent.

1. Lucy/she _____

2. Peter/him _____

3. jacket/it _____

Writing with Pronouns

PRONOUNS: I   me   you   we   us   he   him   it   she   her   they   them

INSTRUCTIONS (PART ONE):

Write a short paragraph without using any pronouns at all. You might want to use pronouns so that your writing doesn't seem awkward (especially toward the end of the paragraph), but control yourself! No pronouns!

_____

_____

_____

_____

INSTRUCTIONS (PART TWO):

Write the same short paragraph, but this time, replace ALL of the nouns in the paragraph with pronouns. This means that you will have an entire paragraph WITHOUT antecedents!

_____

_____

_____

_____

INSTRUCTIONS (PART THREE):

That second paragraph probably didn't make any sense at all because without antecedents, you couldn't figure out what the pronouns were replacing! Now rewrite the paragraph one more time using a nice mix of pronouns and antecedents to make your writing clear.

_____

_____

_____

_____

Grammaropolis

47

The Big Pronoun Quiz!

INSTRUCTIONS: Identify the pronoun in each of the sentences below from the available options.

1. The theater has a little restaurant located behind it.
   O restaurant   O it   O theater   O little

2. Sometimes, I wonder how people can be so inventive.
   O wonder   O people   O I   O inventive

3. You had better write your mother a letter.
   O You   O mother   O your   O better

4. Nadine said she memorized the whole poem!
   O memorized   O she   O Nadine   O poem

5. Kyla and Tashi said, "We are going to stop for lunch."
   O Kyla   O We   O for   O lunch

INSTRUCTIONS: Identify the antecedent (the word the <u>underlined pronoun</u> replaces) from the options below

6. "That dog really likes <u>me</u>," Claire said.
   O Claire   O dog   O that   O really

7. Stephanie, come here. We have some hot soup for <u>you</u>.
   O come   O Stephanie   O we   O here

8. Marisol knows that her friends like <u>her</u> because she is different.
   O she   O Marisol   O different   O friends

9. This book is fascinating. I read <u>it</u> cover to cover.
   O This   O read   O book   O cover

10. Rick said that <u>he</u> would be back by noon.
    O Rick   O noon   O said   O would

Grammaropolis

Meet the Parts of Speech, Grade 1 © 2020 by Grammaropo

Meet the Conjunctions!

EXAMPLES

JOINING WORDS: Billy **and** Joaquin played basketball this morning.

JOINING PHRASES: I usually keep my treasures under the bed **or** in a box.

JOINING COMPLETE THOUGHTS: Nelson's platypus won't bite, **so** you can pet him!

Meet the Parts of Speech, Grade 1 © 2020 by Grammaropolis

Coordinating Conjunctions

Pro Tip:
The FANBOYS (also known as coordinating conjunctions) are used to join **words, phrases,** or **complete thoughts.**

Let's practice!

Instructions:
Circle all of the coordinating conjunctions in the sentences below.

EXAMPLE:

Sylvia slept all day, so she was no longer tired.

1. Traci ate spaghetti and meatballs.

2. You should probably hide under the bed or in the closet.

3. I just had breakfast, but I am already hungry!

4. Cory and his daughter laughed and laughed at my jokes.

5. They should study hard, for the test will be difficult.

Your turn!

Instructions:
Write sentences using the following conjunctions to join words or word groups. Don't forget to circle the conjunction in the sentence!

1. but _____

2. and _____

3. so _____

Meet the Parts of Speech, Grade 1 © 2020 by Grammaropo

Conjunctions Can Join Complete Thoughts

We can use coordinating conjunctions to join two or more complete thoughts into a single sentence.

Without Conjunctions:
I wanted to eat. I went to a restaurant.

With Conjunctions:
I wanted to eat, _so_ I went to a restaurant.

Pro Tip:
A complete thought (also known as an independent clause) makes sense all by itself.

Let's practice!

Instructions:
Join the complete thoughts below into single sentences using the coordinating conjunctions **and, but,** or **so.** Notice how the meaning of your new sentence changes depending on the conjunction you choose!

EXAMPLE:
Soccer is fun, <u>but</u> Jason enjoys basketball more.

1.   My toys are fragile, _____ please be careful.

2.   They are tired, _____ they still want to stay up for the movie.

3.   That shirt is on sale, _____ I will buy it.

4.   The soup is delicious, _____ the crackers are stale.

5.   The moon is full, _____ I don't want to go outside.

Your turn!

Instructions:
Use the following FANBOYS to write sentences with two complete thoughts joined together as a single sentence.

1.   and   _____

2.   so   _____

3.   but   _____

Writing with Conjunctions

COMPLETE THOUGHT BANK

The sky is blue.	The rain fell hard last night.
Tycho is allergic to hot chocolate.	Don't forget to buckle your seat belt.
That car sounds broken.	Fancy cheese can be very expensive.
Kelvin ran across the street.	You learn your own way.
Some people hate lima beans.	I know all the answers.
Toxic chemicals are bad for you.	Reading is important.
Lincoln read quietly.	Willy tripped on the tree root.

COORDINATING CONJUNCTIONS

for   and   nor   but   or   yet   so

INSTRUCTIONS:

Using coordinating conjunctions, write sentences combining any two of the complete thoughts from the complete thought bank into one full sentence, Don't forget to circle the coordinating conjunctions when you use them, and have fun!

EXAMPLE:

Toxic chemicals are bad for you, but fancy cheese can be very expensive.

1. _____

2. _____

3. _____

4. _____

5. _____

Meet the Parts of Speech, Grade 1 © 2020 by Grammaropol

The Big Conjunction Quiz!

INSTRUCTIONS: Identify the conjunction in each of the sentences below from the available options.

1. Maya always writes in green, for it is her favorite color.
   - ○ in
   - ○ for
   - ○ her
   - ○ is

2. The radio station has news, weather, and traffic reports.
   - ○ radio
   - ○ has
   - ○ and
   - ○ reports

3. The park is a favorite spot for rabbits and squirrels.
   - ○ is
   - ○ spot
   - ○ and
   - ○ park

4. Tourists love to visit the site, yet local residents avoid it.
   - ○ to
   - ○ the
   - ○ avoid
   - ○ yet

5. Would you like a burger or fries?
   - ○ Would
   - ○ or
   - ○ you
   - ○ fries

6. You may want to eat that, but I wouldn't do it.
   - ○ but
   - ○ do
   - ○ want
   - ○ eat

7. Spring has not started, yet my flowers are blooming.
   - ○ yet
   - ○ are
   - ○ not
   - ○ has

8. People tend to laugh or cry at my jokes.
   - ○ tend
   - ○ or
   - ○ my
   - ○ at

9. I want to do well in school, so I study hard.
   - ○ to
   - ○ hard
   - ○ so
   - ○ do

10. Over the river and through the woods, to grandmother's house we go!
    - ○ through
    - ○ and
    - ○ go
    - ○ to

Meet the Parts of Speech, Grade 1 © 2020 by Grammaropolis

Meet the Prepositions!

I am a preposition!

I show the relationship between the object (a noun or pronoun) and other words in the sentence.

I help tell where or when something happens.

EXAMPLES

WHERE: They met <u>at</u> the park <u>beside</u> Angie's bicycle.

WHEN: I will wash the dishes <u>in</u> the morning <u>on</u> Tuesday.

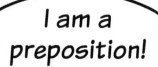

Meet the Parts of Speech, Grade 1 © 2020 by Grammaropo.

Prepositions Help Tell "Where" or "When"

When (time):
I never eat **during** class.

Where (space):
I left a key **under** the welcome mat.

Pro Tip:
A preposition helps tell **when** or **where** something happens by locating an object in time or space.

Let's practice!

Instructions:
Circle the prepositions in the following sentences and then indicate whether each one helps tell when or where the action of the verb happens.

EXAMPLE:

We should go (to) the store.   <u> where </u>

1. I looked under the bed.   _____

2. Please put your dirty dishes in the sink.   _____

3. The stars appear at nighttime.   _____

4. Did you see the fox jump over the creek?   _____

5. Janice promised to do her homework in the morning.   _____

Your turn!

Instructions:
Finish the sentences below by using your own prepositions to tell where or when the action happened. Don't forget to circle the prepositions!

1. <u>Kyle went shopping</u>_____

2. <u>Zeke and I slept</u>_____

3. <u>The whole class read</u>_____

Prepositional Phrases

Pro Tip:
A prepositional phrase starts with a preposition and ends with the object of the preposition.

Let's practice!

Instructions:
In each of the following sentences, underline the entire prepositional phrase and circle the preposition.

EXAMPLE:
Your pencil is (behind) your ear.

1. Thomas walked around the puddle.

2. The Milky Way galaxy shone brightly in the midnight sky.

3. I keep all my comic books under the bed.

4. His cousin played video games for three hours.

5. Oxana looked across the table.

Your turn!

Instructions:
Write sentences that incorporate the prepositional phrases below. Remember to underline the prepositional phrases and circle the prepositions.

1. in the dark _____

2. against the wall _____

3. out the door _____

Writing with Prepositions

INSTRUCTIONS (PART ONE):

Use prepositions from the Preposition Bank to create five prepositional phrases.

PREPOSITION BANK

above	behind	down	near	through
across	below	during	off	throughout
after	beneath	from	on	to
against	beside	in	out	toward
around	between	inside	outside	under
at	beyond	into	over	until
before	by		since	upon

1. _____

2. _____

3. _____

4. _____

5. _____

INSTRUCTIONS (PART TWO):

Now write a sentence for each of your prepositional phrases. Don't forget to circle the prepositions!

1. _____

2. _____

3. _____

4. _____

5. _____

Meet the Parts of Speech, Grade 1 © 2020 by Grammaropolis

The Big Preposition Quiz!

INSTRUCTIONS: Identify the preposition in each of the sentences below from among the available options.

1. The ferns grow well in that damp, cool area.
   - ○ in
   - ○ area
   - ○ cool
   - ○ grow

2. Henry is writing a letter to his grandparents because he loves them.
   - ○ writing
   - ○ his
   - ○ to
   - ○ them

3. The thick moss hung from the grey branches.
   - ○ from
   - ○ grey
   - ○ hung
   - ○ moss

4. Holly spotted a brown lizard lying against a long green leaf.
   - ○ lying
   - ○ a
   - ○ against
   - ○ leaf

5. The students wore jackets over their school uniforms.
   - ○ wore
   - ○ school
   - ○ jackets
   - ○ over

INSTRUCTIONS: Identify the object of the preposition in each of the <u>prepositional phrases underlined</u> below.

6. The cloth features blue whales <u>on a lavender background</u>.
   - ○ background
   - ○ lavender
   - ○ whales
   - ○ cloth

7. Your family always goes on vacation <u>in the last two weeks</u> of summer.
   - ○ family
   - ○ weeks
   - ○ two
   - ○ sumer

8. The frightened bunny hopped <u>across the crowded street</u>.
   - ○ street
   - ○ hopped
   - ○ bunny
   - ○ crowded

9. All of my recipes are <u>in a big black box</u> on the desk.
   - ○ black
   - ○ box
   - ○ desk
   - ○ recipes

10. The country singer signed her contract <u>on the dotted line</u>.
    - ○ dotted
    - ○ singer
    - ○ line
    - ○ contract

Meet the Parts of Speech, Grade 1 © 2020 by Grammaropo

Meet the Interjections!

EXAMPLES

MILD EMOTION: *Gee*, your friends are nice.

STRONG EMOTION: *Yay*! I just wont the lottery!

Meet the Parts of Speech, Grade 1 © 2020 by Grammaropolis

Identifying Interjections

Mild Emotion:
<u>Wow</u>, those potato chips sure are expensive.

Strong Emotion:
<u>Yay</u>! I just won the lottery!

Pro Tip:
*Mild emotion is set apart with a **comma**.*
Strong emotion is set apart with an **exclamation mark***.*

Let's practice!

Instructions:
Circle the interjection in each of the following sentences and indicate whether it is expressing mild or strong emotion.

EXAMPLE:

(Meh,) this could go either way.   mild

1. "Hmmm," she said. "That sounds wrong to me."   _____

2. Oh! That's my favorite candy bar!   _____

3. Um, could you please tell me what is going on here? _____

4. Ouch! That really hurts!   _____

5. C'mon! That wasn't a foul! I hardly touched him! _____

Your turn!

Instructions:
Write sentences using the interjections below to express mild or strong emotion as indicated.

1. Ah (mild)   _____

2. Zowee (strong) _____

3. Eek (strong)   _____

Meet the Parts of Speech, Grade 1 © 2020 by Grammaropo

Writing with Interjections

INSTRUCTIONS (PART ONE):

Write down ten interjections you might use to express mild or strong emotion. Feel free to make up a few of them if you want! Circle your six favorite ones.

1._____   6._____

2._____   7._____

3._____   8._____

4._____   9._____

5._____   10._____

INSTRUCTIONS (PART TWO):

Now write sentences using your favorite interjections. Remember to use a comma when you express mild emotion and an exclamation mark with strong emotion!

MILD EMOTION

1. _____

2. _____

3. _____

STRONG EMOTION:

. _____

2. _____

3. _____

The Big Interjection Quiz!

INSTRUCTIONS: Identify the interjection in each of the sentences below from among the available options.

1. Wow, this cake is good.
   ○ cake   ○ good   ○ Wow   ○ is

2. Oops! I made a mistake on the test.
   ○ test   ○ Oops   ○ on   ○ I

3. Phew! This is an awful lot of work.
   ○ Phew   ○ awful   ○ this   ○ work

4. Uh-oh, it looks like it's starting to rain.
   ○ looks   ○ starting   ○ rain   ○ Uh-oh

5. You got a part in the play! Yay!
   ○ You   ○ play   ○ Yay   ○ part

INSTRUCTIONS: Indicate whether the <u>underlined interjections</u> below express mild emotion or strong emotion.

6. <u>Gee</u>, that's a beautiful painting.
   ○ mild emotion   ○ strong emotion

7. <u>Argh</u>! I hate paper cuts!
   ○ mild emotion   ○ strong emotion

8. <u>Yeah</u>, I can't believe I forgot that.
   ○ mild emotion   ○ strong emotion

9. <u>Oooh</u>! The leaves are turning such beautiful colors!
   ○ mild emotion   ○ strong emotion

10. <u>Shhh</u>, there's no point in talking about that.
    ○ mild emotion   ○ strong emotion

Grammaropolis

Meet the Parts of Speech, Grade 1 © 2020 by Grammarop

The Big Quiz Answer Key!

The Big Noun Quiz!

1. wind
2. band
3. cheeses
4. sunshine
5. grass
6. proper
7. common
8. common
9. proper
10. proper

The Big Pronoun Quiz!

1. it
2. I
3. You
4. she
5. We
6. dog
7. Stephanie
8. Marisol
9. book
10. Rick

The Big Verb Quiz!

1. was
2. sailed
3. feels
4. is
5. went
6. flew
7. knows
8. give
9. will be
10. tied

The Big Conjunction Quiz!

1. for
2. and
3. and
4. yet
5. or
6. but
7. yet
8. or
9. so
10. and

The Big Adjective Quiz!

1. ready
2. fresh
3. hidden
4. long
5. busy
6. breeze
7. dog
8. clouds
9. vegetables
10. paws

The Big Preposition Quiz!

1. in
2. to
3. from
4. against
5. over
6. background
7. weeks
8. street
9. box
10. line

The Big Adverb Quiz!

1. sometimes
2. heavily
3. undoubtedly
4. longingly
5. together
6. read
7. recognized
8. searched
9. smiled
10. secured

The Big Interjection Quiz!

1. Wow
2. Oops
3. Phew
4. Uh-oh
5. Yay
6. mild
7. strong
8. mild
9. strong
10. mild

Grammaropolis

63

GRAMMAR CURRICULUM CHECKLIST

- ☑ Innovative and engaging
- ☑ Aligned to state standards
- ☑ Addresses various learning styles
- ☑ Created and refined in the ultimate proving grounds: the classroom

THE STORYBOOKS

4/24/2019 | $6.99
Paperback | 32 pages | 8" x 8"
Full-color illustrations throughout
Includes instructional back matter
Ages 7 to 11 | Grades 1 to 5
JUVENILE NONFICTION /
LANGUAGE ARTS / GRAMMAR

9781644420157 | Noun
9781644420171 | Verb
9781644420133 | Adjective
9781644420102 | Adverb
9781644420164 | Pronoun
9781644420119 | Conjunction
9781644420140 | Preposition
9781644420126 | Interjection

THE WORKBOOKS

3/03/2020 | $12.99 | B&W
PB | 64 pages | 11"H x 8.5"W
Includes quizzes & instruction
Ages 7 to 11 | Grades 1 to 5
JUVENILE NONFICTION /
LANGUAGE ARTS / GRAMMAR

9781644420300 | Grade 1
9781644420317 | Grade 2
9781644420324 | Grade 3
9781644420331 | Grade 4
9781644420188 | Grade 5

Grammaropolis is available through Ingram Publisher Services.
Contact your IPS Sales Representative to order.
Call (866) 400-5351, Fax (800) 838-1149, ips@ingramcontent.com, or visit ipage.

- An eight-book series starring the parts of speech, which are personified based on the roles they play in the sentence.

- Featuring a different character-based adventure for every part of speech.

- Each book includes standards–aligned definitions and examples, just like you'd find in a textbook (but way more fun).

- Skill-building workbooks featuring character-based instruction along with various comprehension checks and writing exercises.

- Aligned to Common Core and state standards for K–5.

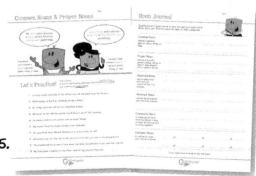

Meet the Parts of Speech, Grade 1 © 2020 by Grammarop...

Printed in the USA
CPSIA information can be obtained
at www.ICGtesting.com
JSHW060239160824
68134JS00058BA/2676

9 781644 42030